For George and our four "babies" with love.
—Paula Spencer

Designed by Heather Zschock

PARENTING is a registered trademark of
The Parenting Group, Inc. Used Under License.

Photo credits appear on page 81

Published by Peter Pauper Press, Inc.
202 Mamaroneck Avenue
White Plains, NY 10601
All rights reserved
ISBN 1-59359-987-0
Printed in China
7 6 5 4 3 2 1

Visit us at www.peterpauper.com

To: MALINI
"MOMMY"
From:
STEVE
"DADDY"

Parentin

The New Mom'
Handbook

Paula Spencer

 PETER PAUPER PRESS, INC.
White Plains, New York

Parenting
The New Mom's Handbook

Contents

"Toasters and flashlights come with more detailed instructions than new babies."

—Ann Douglas

A Whole New World

> "A baby is an angel whose wings decrease as his legs increase."

> —French Proverb

Having a baby is like no other human experience. Maybe that explains why babies can seem so alien at first. Everybody's cooing, "Congratulations!" while you're walking around in a sleepless daze wondering,

"Now what?"

A baby changes everything: your schedule, your priorities,

the way you think about yourself, the way you think about the world. And if you're like most new parents, you have more experience programming your cell phone than deciphering an infant's cries. Even though caring for a baby may feel instinctive at certain moments, you don't automatically become an expert just because now you're some-body's mom! The job takes time and practice.

That said, you're also about to have more fun than a grown-up person ought to! There's nothing like having a baby to bring out the joy and sheer sense of wonder of life (kind of like how we felt when we were children ourselves).

What Babies Need Most

Prompt attention

Don't worry that by tending to your newborn quickly, you'll spoil her. Impossible! Being responsive is essential for her to develop properly. That's how you build her sense of security and confidence. As she gets older (after the first four to six months) you can begin to teach patience. Of course, you should still address her immediate needs right away—hunger, diapering, fatigue, safety—but you needn't rush to give her nonessentials the second she wants them, such as food when she's really not very hungry.

Love

Lucky for you, this is very easy to supply.

No instructions necessary.

Touch

Proven benefits of touch for babies include: crying less, better weight gain, and being more alert. (Research on rats found that even rat pups that were stroked and licked a lot grew up to be smarter!)

So hold, cuddle, carry, rock, pat, and love your baby—plenty.

Play

This is how babies learn. Anything that stimulates your child's senses and helps him figure out how the world works qualifies as play. This can include listening to you sing, waving a rattle, looking into a mirror, gnawing a board book, watching the clouds, and flicking mushy peas over a high chair. You don't even need to buy a lot of fancy toys (unless you can't resist).

What New Parents Need Most

Patience

It took nine months to grow a baby; now it can take at least that long to grow comfortable as a parent. Your baby's timetable and pace won't always match your own. Surrendering control can be a challenge. Keep doing that Lamaze breathing you learned in childbirth class—it will come in handy when your stress level is high and your patience runs low!

Humor

You open a diaper and your son squirts you. Your daughter decides to shampoo her hair with her yogurt. Your house looks like a tornado has moved in—what should you do? Laugh!

Help!

Enlist friends and relatives to run errands or watch the baby. Accept all those casseroles the neighbors bring. Consider hiring a postpartum *doula*, a professional who helps with baby care—and babies *you*. Join (or start) a babysitting co-op and a moms' group. (Hint: Playgroups aren't about socializing the babies; they're about providing the moms with like-minded

company and much-needed con-
versation!)

Consider the advice in this
little guidebook to be an extra
pair of hands to ease your way.

New parents not only
need all the help they
can get, they deserve it.

Baby's Greatest Hits

Some developmental milestones to look forward to:

STARTS TO SMILE: **1 to 2 months**

STARTS TO COO: **2 to 4 months**

GRASPS A RATTLE: **3 to 4 months**

SITS UP (WITH A BIT OF PROPPING):
4 to 5 months

ROLLS OVER: **3 to 5 months**

FIRST TOOTH: **5 to 10 months**

SITS UP (UNSUPPORTED):
6 to 7 months

CRAWLS: **6 to 8 months**

STANDS, HOLDING ON: **7 to 9 months**

SAYS "MAMA," AND "DADA":
9 to 11 months

STANDS ALONE: **10 to 11 months**

FIRST WORD (AFTER "MAMA"):
11 to 12 months

FIRST STEPS: **10 to 14 months**

Babies vary in their development; these guidelines are only approximations. In other words, enjoy the accomplishments, but don't stress if they occur later rather than sooner.

CHAPTER 1

Sleeping

(It's Not an Elusive Dream!)

"The art of being a parent is to sleep when the baby isn't looking."

—Anonymous

How is it that babies get so much sleep, but parents don't seem to get any? Part of the problem is that newborns start out not knowing day from night. It takes them about six weeks to get on a schedule when they're sleeping for one longer stretch at night in addition to a few daytime naps. As it is, that stretch—rather optimistically named "sleeping through the night"—lasts only four to six hours. Even then, your baby may wake two or three times a night for the first six months.

Where your baby sleeps is mostly a matter of preference and safety. A Moses basket or cradle is fine, but only big enough for the first few months. "My son would sleep in his car seat and nowhere else," says Kelly Johnson, mom of two in Clinton, Tennessee. "We'd put his car seat in the bassinet beside our bed and he'd sleep like an angel." Some moms use a crib right from the start. If you do, consider putting a day bed or twin bed in the nursery where you can crash if necessary, especially when your baby is young or sick. Keep the crib free of pillows and toys, which are a smothering risk.

Most safety experts don't recommend sleeping with your baby in your bed, but if you do, be sure you have a firm mattress (no waterbeds) and keep blankets away from your baby's face.

For safety's sake, always put your baby to sleep on her back wherever she sleeps.

Sleep Timeline
Perchance to Dream

1 week: TOTAL SLEEP: **16 ½ hrs.**
DAY SLEEP: **8 hrs.**
NIGHT SLEEP: **8 ½ hrs.**

1 month: TOTAL SLEEP: **15 ½ hrs.**
DAY SLEEP: **7 hrs.**
NIGHT SLEEP: **8 ½ hrs.**

3 months: TOTAL SLEEP: **15 hrs.**
DAY SLEEP: **5 hrs.**
NIGHT SLEEP: **10 hrs.**

6 months: TOTAL SLEEP: **14 $\frac{1}{4}$ hrs.**
DAY SLEEP: **3 $\frac{1}{4}$ hrs.**
NIGHT SLEEP: **11 hrs.**

9 months: TOTAL SLEEP: **14 hrs.**
DAY SLEEP: **3 hrs.**
NIGHT SLEEP: **11 hrs.**

12 months: TOTAL SLEEP: **13 $\frac{3}{4}$ hrs.**
DAY SLEEP: **2 $\frac{1}{4}$ hrs.**
NIGHT SLEEP: **11 $\frac{1}{2}$ hrs.**

Insider Tips for Getting the Little One to Sleep

Swaddle a newborn snugly in a receiving blanket.

Being wrapped up at bedtime makes a little baby feel secure and more calm: It's like being in the womb again.

Wake her up before you lay her down.

Sounds counterintuitive, doesn't it? But if you put your baby into bed drowsy, rather than after she's out cold, she learns to drift off on her own. Then when she wakes up briefly in the night—as all humans do—she's more likely to settle back to sleep without your help.

Keep it consistent.

"I never lived with a schedule before in my life, but I live by my son's schedule now," says Susan Herrera of Fort Polk, Louisiana. "I love him, but I love him a lot more when he's happy, and keeping to a schedule keeps him that way." Reinforce sleep-wake patterns by having your baby feed, play, nap, and go to bed at roughly the same time every day (after about three to four months).

Be proactive.

Don't wait until your baby is
rubbing her eyes, yawning, and
crying to put her down; by then
she's already overtired.

Be "un-fun" at night.

If you must change a middle-of-
the-night diaper or check out a
cry, be businesslike. Too much
talk or play is stimulating. The
less you chat, cuddle, or play with
your baby in the wee hours, the

more he will learn to associate night with sleep.

Set the mood.

Keep the room dark and turn on lullabies or white noise. These "sleep cues" tell your baby it's Z-time, the way the feel of your favorite pillow works for you.

Develop a predictable bedtime routine.

One example: bathing, nursing,

reading or rocking, singing lullabies, tucking in. Keep it short (under a half-hour) and sweet.

Remember to breathe.

"If you get frustrated or annoyed with a crying baby, that baby knows," says Lindsay Barrett of Kansas City, Kansas. You can't always be Zen-like, but remember that babies pick up on the tension around them. On the other hand, they pick up on the good vibes, too.

Insider Tips for Getting the Big One (You!) to Sleep

Resist not the number-one new mom cliché: "Sleep when the baby sleeps." Enough said.

Rely on freshness, not fakes.

A double latte may pep you up or a glass of merlot may ease your evening, but ultimately

both mess up your sleep cycles.
On the other hand, even brief
exercise or being outside pays off
later. "A breath of fresh air and a
change of scenery not only buys
me five minutes of calm, it can be
enough to recharge me for a long
night ahead," says Cynthia
Villines, a mom of two in
Riverside, California.

Arrange help.
Add precious minutes to your

sleep total by depending on others, like rotating night duty with Dad. Try some unconventional methods, like hiring a babysitter just so you can nap, or trading off with a friend who also has a baby.

Lower your standards.

Nobody will think less of you if you leave dirty dishes in the sink longer than usual, order take-out, or let dust collect like snowdrifts. Visitors just want to see your baby.

TOOLS OF THE TRADE:
SLEEPING

- Crib with firm mattress
- Fitted sheets (cotton or flannel)
- Crib bumpers (firm, not fluffy)
- Plush musical toys (like giraffes or bears) that you pull to make music
- Musical mobiles suspended over crib (until baby can stand)
- Unbreakable mirror (to attach to side of crib)
- White noise machine or soft lullaby music
- Swing
- Pacifier

Sleeping Troubleshooter

If your baby won't stop crying:

If he's not hungry or needing a diaper change, and he's older than five months, try "Ferberizing": Let him cry for five minutes. Come back and rub his back or talk to him for two or three minutes. Leave for five minutes. Repeat, leaving for progressively longer periods. The idea: to teach him to fall asleep on his own.

If your baby misses a nap:
See if she'll take one later than
usual. If she hasn't slept by din-
nertime, just put her to bed for
the night earlier than usual.

**If your routines are ruined by
vacation or sickness:** Just go
back to your old schedule instead
of continuing the new pattern.
Sleep patterns are easily disrupt-
ed, but the good news is that
they're easily re-learned.

If your baby wakes up before the roosters: Delay responding to him for a few minutes (if he's older than five months). Gradually he may learn to amuse himself or go back to sleep. With an older baby, leave board books or a few safe toys in the crib to discover in the wee hours of the morning.

CHAPTER 2

Feeding

(Again, and Again, and Again!)

"Nothing in parenting is as rewarding as a big, wet burp after a feeding."

—T. Berry Brazelton, MD

Feeding time isn't just about nourishment. It's also a delicious opportunity to snuggle, relax, and bond. As your baby gets older, mealtimes are a chance for him to explore and learn.

Which "first food" will you choose? Breast-feeding is convenient (you can do it anywhere, with no bottles to clean) and low cost (it's free!), and breast milk contains the perfect mix of nutrients, antibodies, and other protective substances, customized for your baby. It's also easy to digest and reduces the chances of allergy. That's why many doctors recommend breast-feeding for the first few weeks at least, if you can, and ideally continuing for the first twelve months of life. If you can't do either of those things, though, you can rest assured that modern formulas provide fine nutrition. You can't go wrong either way.

What's for Dinner Mom?

BIRTH TO 4–6 MONTHS: Feed with breast milk or formula only

4 TO 6 MONTHS: Introduce cereal (first rice or oats)

6 TO 9 MONTHS: Introduce other solids (first fruits and vegetables, in either order, then proteins)

8 TO 12 MONTHS: Begin weaning from bottle to cup, begin self-feeding

12 MONTHS: Introduce whole milk

Insider Tips for Feeding Your Baby

Dress the part.

"I borrowed a couple of tops and a dress made for nursing moms with special openings," says Patti Anderson of Cincinnati. "Quick access is a lifesaver when your baby is hungry." Toss a baby blanket over your shoulder if you want more privacy.

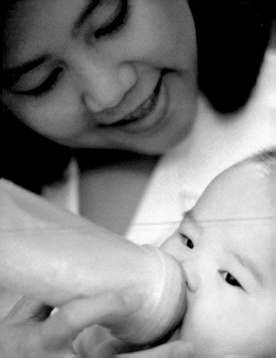

Introduce a bottle early.

Even if you plan to breast-feed exclusively, it pays to get your baby used to a bottle in the first month of life, after your milk supply is established. This will make it possible for someone else to occasionally offer a bottle of expressed milk, allowing you to get out of the house—or sleep! Some moms alternate breast milk and formula when their babies are older.

Set the table.

Once your baby can sit up and eat solids, serve meals at the high chair. Putting her in the chair becomes her cue it's chowtime.

Make like a scout: Be prepared.

"Don't put the baby in the high chair until you have all food warmed, in bowls and dishes, with silverware ready," says Kristen Cotter of Lancaster, New York, mom of Chandler Ann. "This way she won't get upset while she waits." Bonus: You can devote your full attention to the meal.

Share.

Once your baby is ready for table food, consider grinding or dicing whatever the family is having. "Clay thinks things are more interesting when we share them off my plate," says Wanda Celgin, a mother in Arnold, Maryland.

What Not to Feed a Baby—and Why

HONEY: Risk of botulism in infants

COW'S MILK: Not digestible

WHEAT (BEFORE 6-12 MONTHS):
Possible allergen

PEANUT BUTTER, TREE NUTS,
CITRUS, SHELLFISH, EGG WHITES
(BEFORE 1-3 YEARS): Possible allergens

POPCORN, RAW CARROTS,
HOT DOGS (UNLESS FINELY DICED),
STRING CHEESE, WHOLE GRAPES,
LOLLIPOPS, RAISINS, MARSHMALLOWS:
Choking hazards

Feeding Troubleshooter

If you're on the go: Stash nonperishables in your diaper bag: jars of baby food, snacks such as individually-wrapped biter biscuits or crackers, and ready-to-pour formula.

If your baby is messy: Be proud. You have a scientist in training! Babies smash, smear, drop, and throw food as a way of exploring and learning. Spread newspaper, a shower curtain, or a splat mat under the high chair.

If your baby is a fussy eater:
Don't worry if she goes gaga for cottage cheese day after day, but turns up her nose at the other foods you offer. Nutritionists say you may have to introduce a new food as many as ten to twelve times before a child will try it. She may smell it, touch it, or play with it for many meals before she

actually consents to eat it.

If your baby doesn't seem to eat a balanced diet: Be sure you're looking at his diet across a week, not on a given day or at a given meal. As long as you are offering a broad range of choices, the nutrition is apt to even out over time. Few modern babies develop scurvy or protein deficiencies!

If your baby doesn't seem interested in eating: Food is pretty much just an energy source to an infant. They don't attach all the emotional and social ties to it that grown-ups have. During growth spurts, a baby's appetite can be ravenous. Then the growth slows, and so does the consumption. If you're really concerned, mention it to your doctor. Plotting your baby's weight gain on a growth chart can reassure you that all's well.

TOOLS OF THE TRADE:
FEEDING

Beginners:

- Burp cloths
- Bottles
- Nipples
- Brushes to wash bottles and nipples
- Breast pump
- Basket for dishwasher (to hold bottle rings and nipples)
- Rocking chair

week. (That's why there are wet wipes.) It's really your call.

Baths do more than get your baby smelling sweet again. They're playtime. They can calm fussiness and be a prelude to sleep. And there's nothing like splashing in warm water and caressing those plump baby limbs to calm a frazzled mom, too.

Bath Timeline
Rub-a-Dub-Tub

UNTIL UMBILICAL CORD SITE
HEALS:
sponge bath only

UNTIL BABY CAN SIT UNSUP-
PORTED:
baby bathtub or sink

REST OF CHILDHOOD:
regular bathtub

Insider Tips for Soothing Baths

Make tub time something to look forward to.

You probably find regular showers or soaks relaxing; so will your baby. "I gave my daughter a bath every night it was possible. It became part of the bedtime routine," says Melissa Hildebrand of Broadway, Virginia, mom of Cameron.

Give it your full attention.

Collect all your supplies, including several towels, ahead of time. (One towel warms the baby and does an initial dry-off; then you can wrap her in the second dry towel.) Keep the room warm. Never take a hand off your baby for a second. Let the phone and doorbell ring.

Stimulate baby's senses.

"With each of our kids, we always put the baby tub on the counter in the bathroom with the biggest mirror to allow the baby to see himself in the mirror," says Laura Patyk, a mom of six in Indian Trail, North Carolina. "Also after about two months we use lavender baby wash. Something about the lavender aroma seems to soothe them—and me!"

Don't forget the rubber duckies.

Make baths fun. Lift your baby's hand to touch and splash the water. Provide cups to fill and pour. Sing!

End with a rubdown.

Sounds heavenly, doesn't it? Babies love massage. It's soothing and provides the comforting benefits of skin-to-skin contact. After you dry your baby off, rub a little bit of lotion into your hands. (Remove your rings.) Stroke her back, limbs, and tummy gently, but with firm pressure.

TOOLS OF THE TRADE:
BATHING

- Baby tub (before baby can sit up)

- Bath seat (after baby can sit up unsupported)

- Soft, small washcloths

- Baby-safe soap and shampoo

- Hooded towel

- Washable rubber bath toys

CONCLUSION
Hang In There!

"Your top job as a new
parent is to love your
baby like crazy."

—Harvey Karp, MD

Parenting is a work in progress. You'll have great days, and you'll have others where you look at the clock every five minutes and wonder how you'll ever make it to tomorrow, let alone kindergarten. The good news is that you're learning something every day, and sooner than you think, it won't seem so intimidating or strange.

"My mother used to tell me that she was put on this earth to be my mother," says Jennifer Martin of Brandon, Mississippi. "Only now that I'm a parent myself can I appreciate that. I was put here to be Catie's mom and I can imagine no greater gift."

Before long you will look at your great big baby—or toddler, or preschooler, or college graduate—and wonder where the time flew!

Probably one of the biggest gifts you can give to both yourself and your baby is to let go of as much stress as you can. Picture each stressor (a sleepless night, spilled cereal, too much advice from well-meaning people) like a big droplet of water and let it roll off your back. Another tactic for when you're feeling overwhelmed: Take a deep breath and gaze into your baby's eyes. That's all that really matters. Right there.

> "The hand that rocks the cradle Is the hand that rules the world."

—William Ross Wallace